When
GOD
Made the
DAKOTAS

Tim Kessler   Paul Morin

Eerdmans Books for Young Readers
Grand Rapids, Michigan • Cambridge, U.K.

To the North Fourth Street Writers Group: Clem, Janet, and Mary
— *T. K.*

To Kadin and to the Creator for his gifts
— *P. M.*

Text Copyright © 2006 Timothy Kessler
Images Copyright © 2006 Paul Morin
Published in 2006 by Eerdmans Books for Young Readers
An imprint of Wm. B. Eerdmans Publishing Company
255 Jefferson S.E., Grand Rapids, Michigan 49503
P.O. Box 163, Cambridge CB3 9PU U.K.
www.eerdmans.com / youngreaders

Manufactured in China
06 07 08 09 10 11   8 7 6 5 4 3 2 1
Library of Congress Cataloging-in-Publication Data

Kessler, Timothy.
When God made the Dakotas / written by Timothy Kessler ; illustrated by Paul Morin.
p. cm.
ISBN 0-8028-5275-0 (alk. paper)
1. Dakota mythology. 2. Creation–Mythology. I. Morin, Paul, 1959- ill. II. Title.
E99.DIK47 2005
299.7'85243013–dc22

The text and display type is set in Albertus.
The illustrations were created with acrylic on canvas on cedar stretchers.
The colors used were inspired by the landscape and atmosphere of the Dakotas.
Gayle Brown, Art Director
Matthew Van Zomeren, Graphic Designer
Cover design by Paul Morin

When
GOD
Made the
DAKOTAS

Late in the afternoon of the First Day, the Great Spirit, Wakantanka, came to the final empty place. Woksape, the medicine man of the Dakotas, was waiting for him.

"Welcome, Great Spirit," said the medicine man, "Are you come now to make a land for my people?"

"Yes, Woksape, Old Friend," replied Wakantanka. "I am come to fashion a land for the Dakotas. From the contents I carry here in Wohuza, my medicine bag, I will create the Dakota Nation. However," he continued, dropping his bag to the ground, "let me rest for a bit. I have made an entire world, and I am exceedingly tired. While I rest, you can think about the sort of land you want for your people."

"I have been thinking of nothing else," said Woksape.

They sat then, as was their fashion, cross-legged on the rim of the earth. Woksape saw that Wakantanka's moccasins were dusty and stained with much travel. He saw too that Wohuza, the medicine bag, hung limp and without much weight. Cannonpa, the Sacred Pipe, rested in Wakantanka's beaded belt, and the three white feathers of his headdress grew gray in the late day sun.

When he had rested for a length of the sun, Wakantanka spoke.

"I am ready, Old Friend. Tell me what sort of land you would like for your people."

Woksape rose respectfully to his feet and spoke these words:

"Oh, Great Spirit, the Dakotas would like a land of great stone mountains whose jagged peaks are topped with the snow of many winters, mountains where flashing trout spawn in fast rushing streams, and whose meadows team with bear and elk, a land like you have given to our brothers to the West, the Shoshone and the Flathead."

Wakantanka opened the bag and peered inside. He set the bag down slowly, shaking his head.

"I'm sorry, Old Friend," he said quietly. "I have no mountains left to give. Some gently sloping hills, a few bluffs, are all that remain. Ask for something else."

Woksape thought quietly for a moment and then spoke these words:

"Oh, Great Spirit, if we cannot have mountains that pierce the sky, then give to the Dakotas a land of great boreal forests, a land ever green with the tall spruce and fir and pine, under whose shade deer and moose and fox and lynx grow fat, a land like you have given to our brothers to the North, the Chipewyan and the Cree."

Again, Wakantanka looked into his bag. Again, he slowly shook his head.

"I'm indeed sorry, Old Friend, but I have none of the giant forests left to give. All that remain are a few leafy cottonwoods and these grasses. Ask for something else."

This time, Woksape remained quiet even longer. He then spoke these words:

"Oh, Great Spirit, if the Dakotas cannot have mountains or great green forests that shade the earth, then give to us a land of many lakes and a great freshwater sea full of fish to eat, a land lined with many rivers and tributaries where the otter and the beaver build their homes, a land such as you have given to our brothers to the East, the Anishinabe and the Winnebago."

Wakantanka peered deeply into his medicine bag. Slowly, he raised his eyes and looked at the small man standing before him.

"Old Friend, again I am sorry. The great inland seas, like the mountains and the forests, have all been taken. I have but a few shallow lakes and a dozen small streams. Ask for something else."

The medicine man of the Dakotas was silent for a very long time. He then spoke these words:

"Oh, Great Spirit, if the Dakotas cannot have mountains or forests or seas where schools of fish swim in countless numbers, then give to us a land of desert beauty and sunshine, a land of brightly colored rocks and canyons, a land where the sun shines every day and it is always warm, a land rich in sheep and goats, a land such as you have given to our brothers to the South, the Hopi, the Navajo, and the Apache.

This time, the Great Spirit did not even have to look in his bag. He shook his great head from side to side.

"Woksape, I am truly sorry. I no longer have any land like that left to give. All that remain are a few rocks with hues of red and gold, of yellow and purple. One last time, Old Friend, ask for something else."

Woksape, the medicine man of the Dakotas, sat down on the rim of the world and gazed at the sun setting on the new world. He was silent for a very long time. Finally, Woksape got to his feet and, opening his arms in supplication before the Creator, he spoke these words:

"Oh, Great Spirit, it is you who have made all that is. All who walk the earth know your generosity. You are great and wonderful and loving. Give to your people, the Dakotas, whatever you have left to give and it will be good."

"Woksape," Wakantanka said. "your speech has gladdened my heart. Now, listen and watch as I create the land of the Dakotas from what remains in my bag."

Wakantanka turned the bag upside down and shook the contents onto the ground before him. He picked up all the colored rocks and, as he spoke, he ground the rocks into dust in the palms of his hands.

"I no longer have a desert land of colorful rocks and canyons to give you, a land of constant sunshine where it is always warm. Your land will be a land of many seasons, hot in summer, cold in winter, and sometimes harsh to train my faithful. But at the end of every day, I will give my smile to the sunset."

He lifted his hands and blew the dust in his palms into the western sky. "It will be most radiant, the most colorful sunset of anywhere on earth. In all seasons, it will warm your soul."

The Great Spirit next picked up the small remaining lakes and rivers. He also picked up the green grasses. He rolled them all together in the palm of his hand and sang softly to them. Wakantanka then divided the waters and placed them sparingly on the land. The grasses, however, he spread broadly across the land.

"You asked for a great inland sea and many lakes teeming with fish to eat, a land that I no longer have to give. I will give you something better. I will cover the land of the Dakotas in tall prairie grasses. I have taught the grasses the song of the sea, and it is in their bending and swaying, their restless, waving undulation, that you will see and feel the motion of the distant sea.

The Great Spirit blew his breath across the grass-covered land, and it rippled like a thing alive.

"Further," said Wakantanka, "from the skin of my medicine bag, Wohuza, I will fashion for the Dakotas a special animal to swim in this ocean of grass."

In the hands of the Great Spirit, the medicine bag itself was lovingly reworked into the sturdy, shaggy buffalo.

"This is Tatanka," he said, setting the animal into the grass. "He will multiply into tens and hundreds and thousands and millions. I will teach him to run in herds larger than the largest school of fish. He will become your living medicine bag for in him you will find everything you need to live. His bones will give you tools; his hide, clothing and shelter; his meat will fill your stomachs.

The hands of the Great Spirit next picked up the leathery-leafed cottonwood trees and planted them along the watercourses. Finishing, he took Cannonpa, the sacred pipe, from his belt. He lit the pipe and began to smoke.

"You asked for the shade of the great boreal forests. I have none left to give. I will give you something better." Wakantanka puffed on his pipe and a great cloud of white smoke rose in the air. "For your shade," he said, "I give you these sacred clouds. Not only will they cool the land beneath them, but they will also bring the rain to feed the grasses, which will feed the buffalo, which will feed you. And," he added, "I will form these clouds into shapes that will delight your eyes and instruct your spirit."

All that remained now from the contents of Wakantanka's medicine bag were the small hills and bluffs. Wakantanka placed the hills so that, from east to west, the land of the Dakotas gently rose and fell as if imitating the swells of a giant sea.

When he had finished, Wakantanka quietly pondered his work. After a few moments of silence, Wakantanka took the two outer feathers from his headdress and began to fashion them as he spoke.

"You asked for jagged mountains, and I had only these few hills remaining," said the Great Spirit. "But now I will give you something better. What your land lacks in height, I will make up for in breadth. Yours will be a vast land, a land that looks like eternity." Wakantanka opened his cupped hands and made a haunting cry over the feathers lying there. A large bird appeared.

"This is Maga, the mighty goose," Wakantanka said. He lifted Maga high into the sky and immediately the goose began to multiply. "Maga and his children, who are the heralds of the seasons, will fly overhead every spring and every fall. I will teach them to fly in the shape of a mountain, to make the shape of a mountain peak for my people the Dakotas, to show them how big is my love for this land. And, so all nations and all peoples everywhere know that I honor this land, I will teach them this song."

The flock of geese, which had become huge in the sky, wheeled towards them, forming a giant vee. As they drew closer, Woksape, the medicine man of the Dakotas, could hear them singing —

God loves the Dakotas.
God loves the Dakotas.

Woksape was so happy that he thought his heart would break for joy. But then Wakantanka spoke once more.

"I have one more special gift for the Dakotas," said Wakantanka. "My promise is that I will never let this land become so full of people and their doings that it will drown out the sound of my voice. Here, in the broad vastness of the prairies, you will always be able to hear me, whispering to your heart and bringing you peace."

And so the two sat, side by side, and watched the end of the day, as the radiant sunset smiled through the clouds, and the buffalo drifted in the waving grass, and the geese in the shape of jagged peaks flew overhead singing.

And it was good.